Keanna Green Presents:

Life's
Reckoning

VOLUME I: Why Not Me?
A comprehensive workbook series for life management

Copyright Pending © 2021 Keanna Green and Vision Life Consulting Services.
Copyright Cerebral IP Docket: 0012021CCP
Copyright Case Number: 1-103331586809

All rights reserved. No part of this publication may be reproduced, distributed, or transmitted in any form or by any means, including photocopying, recording, or other electronic or mechanical methods, without prior written permission of the publisher, except in the case of brief quotations embodied in critical reviews and certain other noncommercial uses permitted by copyright law. For permission requests, write to the publisher, addressed "Attention Permissions Coordinator" at the address below.

P.O BOX 365221
Hyde Park, Ma, 02136

ISBN: 978-1-953209-00-9   (Paperback)
ISBN: 978-1-953209-06-1   (E-Book)

Any reference to historical events, real people, or real places are used in context with credit and or permission. Names, people and places are products of the author's personal experience perspective and understanding on public figures, events or current world affairs.

Front cover image by Keanna Green
Book design by Keanna Green
First Printing Edition 2021
Vision Life Consulting Services
visionlifeservices@gmail.com

This series is dedicated to my lineage, ancestors, and those who have come before me; the support and love of those with me now; and the promise and hope of the love and relations that will come tomorrow. Namaste.

They say don't judge a book by its cover. But here's my judgment of the cover.
Photographer Keanna Green
Cover Title Tropical Treasures

Tourists come to the island. and take treasures of their choice. While giving little acknowledgment, nor a listening ear, to the island's honest voice. The voice of the people, indigenous and proud. The same ones who say, "we don't need your listening ears, because we are bossy and load. We sing with a lion's roar and speak from the heart. Our bond as people will not be torn apart. One out of many, is the mantra of our land. We will migrate and spread out, but united we stand.

Complete your collection with all six volumes in this workbook series.

- 💡 **Vol 1 - Why Not You?**
- 💡 **Vol 2 - Who Loves Who?**
- 💡 **Vol 3 - Stress**
- 💡 **Vol 4 - Life's Business Plan**
- 💡 **Vol 5 - The Art of Happiness**
- 💡 **Vol 6 - Activity Workbook**

FOREWORD

This book is about taking personal responsibility. A simple act that can have lifechanging results.
Growing up in Jamaica, I was always taught "yuh reap wha you sow" (you reap what you sow). That phrase acted as a constant reminder that one day, I would face a day of reckoning. We all would. On that day, we would have to take personal responsibility for our actions, whether we wanted to or not. *Life's Reckoning* is about doing this work. It is necessary if we want to live our best lives.

The first volume in this work, "Why Not You?", focuses on delving into questions about your self-image. Keanna will lead you through analysis while encouraging you to face certain truths. At times, you will find yourself shattering the happy. You will discover that you are the holder of secrets. Secrets that will take you to happy spaces but will also remind you of the pain. Pain that has left you wounded. But through discovery, you will learn that you hold the power to redemption.

Continuing down the path of discovery, the second volume is titled "Who Loves Who?" and focuses on self-love, the only form of love that you wholeheartedly control. When you are in control, you can steer your own ship and become the master of your own fate. As you grapple with confusion, you will become more confident in the knowledge that you are reclaiming your power. The power to be you. Keanna does not allow you to simply sit with the negative; she uses it to show you your strength.

The third volume asks you to examine the role of stress in your life. Keanna does not allow you to simply identify the adversity but rather further understanding why it is also important. Explore the concept of positive and negative stressors. Awareness promotes a path that leads to strength in self. Motivators to overcome and accomplish life goals.

"Creating Your Life's Business Plan," volume four, shows you how to create a vision for your life on many meaningful levels. This allows you to create, and dictate, your own path to success. Keanna again asks the important questions that allow you to delve into your truth, and the visual collage in this book strengthens your resolve as you do so. Finally, in volume five, Keanna works with you to examine "The Art of Happiness." I can guarantee that the process of completing this final chapter leads to fulfillment. It leads to the freedom to walk in your truth. It allows your heart to sing. It gives you the conviction to follow your life plan and make the choices that are best for you, unapologetically.

Life's Reckoning has even motivated me to self-reflect, and I was originally Keanna's teacher! But it was a pleasure being her student. I am proud to have walked this journey with Keanna. I respect the hard work that Keanna has done to bring her to this place, and the fact that she has created the opportunity for you to develop your own blueprint to success. Accept her invitation and take the plunge into self-actualization. You are worth it. Irie! (It is all good!)

Mabel Reid-Wallace, M. Ed.

A Note from the Author:

As a Jamerican, duality is the foundation of my existence. My work always includes Jamaican proverbs and translations. They allow me to highlight concepts and notions of importance. Allow this guide to take you away, without catching a flight. Know that acknowledging what is wrong can actually be right. Have the most profound conversation, all by yourself. And know this supports your mental and emotional health. Irie!

Suggested tools and resources for a complete interactive experience

- All five volumes of *Life's Reckoning* and the *Life's Reckoning Activity Workbook*
- A writing utensil
- Access to a music player
- Access to a kitchen
- Access to groceries listed in recipes
- An open mind

Vision Life Consulting Services Resident DJ, The Immortal DJ Spoogie

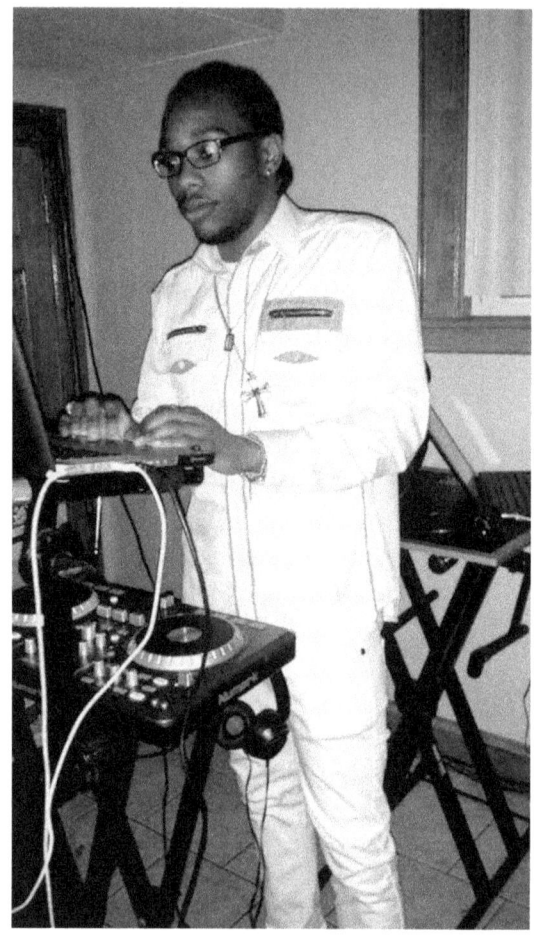

Musical inspiration for this volume is Dennis Brown's 1977 song, "Here I Come."

Here I come with love and not hatred

Surely goodness and mercy shall follow I

All the days of my life

Fall in love with the best version of yourself.

Do it now sometimes later becomes never.

Take time with yourself to make your soul happy.

Believe in yourself and keep on going for you.

Your biggest commitment must always be yourself.

Change your thoughts and you change everything.

Don't regret your past learn from it.

Do more of what makes you happy.

Volume I: Why Not You?

Disclaimer

This guide does not aim to dispel right from wrong. Instead, it aims to be the beginning of a journey of self-exploration. It is presumed that this work is done while gravitating towards a positive, productive disposition, fully taking in the experience of being alive vs. existing, and accepting the mere fact that in this moment, you are ALIVE. With that, there is always opportunity to start anew. May your journey into self be enlightened through LOVE.

Most are unaware that their behavior can be linked to the long-term effects of systemic desensitization. We are desensitized to certain concepts and emotions surrounding self-image, love and relationships. Critical thinking, which is the process of digesting information, is the first concept to consider. We are the sum of our experiences both good and bad. The experiences that result in the most extreme emotions tend to resonate with us long after an event has taken place. These events hare stored in our subconscious and are often referred to as memories. Memories and past experiences are the information initially called upon in our decision-making process. Taking the time to regularly check in and self-evaluate the overall perspective of the subconscious is critical to making both efficient and effective decisions for yourself. A simple check starts with basic questions. For example, "Are you happy?" Evaluate that question relative to your current status and future goals. Can you see yourself reaching your goals if you stay on your current path? Are you maintaining a positive mental attitude?

From cow nuh dead, him wi shake em' tail. ⇔ *From cow not dead, he will shake his tail.*

While there is life, there is hope!

Mental Break

A simple self-check

Are you happy?

List some past experiences and memories that resonate with you today:

How have these memories influenced your present life? Have they had positive or negative impacts?

Can you see yourself reaching your goals if you continue on your current path? Why or why not?

Are you maintaining a positive mental attitude?

___

Most life problems can be remedied with what I call the Inside Out Method. The process is initiated with an informed perspective of the individual self. The first step in resolving issues begins with you. Start working from the inside by focusing on your mental and emotional health. You'll need a holistic, balanced perspective. This includes honest evaluation of who you are, where you are and where you would like to be. When you accept and digest your experience from a neutral perspective, considering both the good with the bad, you'll uncover information that is critical to your growth. Repetition and consciously noting the positive vs. the negative experiences will impart wisdom. Even in a seemingly bad situation, you can find your silver lining. Moving forward, you may not have gained the results you anticipated. And that's okay. What you will have gained is the ability to learn *how* to achieve the results you desire. Over time, you'll notice you have a stronger relationship with yourself as you become your own trusted expert on all matters regarding you. You will feel more confident "following your first mind." Beginning this process will enable you to start creating a mental road map or a life plan.

Bird cyaan fly pon one wing. ⇔ *A bird cannot fly on one wing.*

There is no good without bad. (Balance is necessary.)

Let's examine the concept of lying. The act of lying has a negative connotation and signifies a deficiency, an evasion of reality. A well-rounded individual demonstrates honest, balanced evaluation of oneself, and the overall situation. When this practice becomes a process of habit, decision-making is sounder and more holistic. These concerted decisions will propel you towards your desired life outcomes. When you are honest with yourself and those around you, you have identified a real starting point. A starting point for creating parameters around healthy relationships and life goals. As well as a starting point to activate and aid the process of life barrier identification and removal. A neutral perspective and acceptance that life will give you both good and bad runs parallel with realization. Awareness that duality is the essence of life. Life does not exist with one and not the other. Whether or not your current perspective allows you to identify opposition is irrelevant to its presence. Failing to acknowledge it does not eliminate its existence. This unacknowledged opposition manifests into unexpected roadblocks which can throw you off kilter. Finding your zero point — or balance — in life is imperative to a positively holistic and equitable life experience.

The only guarantees in life are birth and death. Thinking about this reality can reduce stress. When you accept the notion that death is a natural part of life, as you move forward, you begin perfecting the ability to live more efficiently. The personal selection process becomes refined as your desire to waste time, effort or energy wanes. Giving way to mentally digest other aspects. Consider this: what will you do with the time you have left? Who are you today? Where are you today? Who and where do you want to be tomorrow? And if you did pass on, what would your legacy be? When you make decisions using discernable facts, and not merely emotions, you begin working smarter, not harder. Use the blessing of time and energy to accomplish things that will have profound positive impacts created for you, by you.

Tek weh yuh get, till yuh get weh yuh want. ⇔ *Take what you get until you get what you want.*

Every opportunity should be used as a stepping stone towards manifesting your ultimate goal.

Mental Break

Who are you? (Include how you identify culturally, ethnically and spiritually.)

Where are you today?

Who and where would you like to be in the future?

What is your life's objective?

How we deal with the good and bad in life matters. Tremendously. For most of us, if it's not one thing, it's another. We all go through it. Despite these basic truths, we often ask ourselves, "why me?" But maybe a better question is, if not you, then who?

Putting more emphasis on the resolution, as opposed to the problem, helps you avoid wasting time with questions like "why me?" It also contributes to a positive mental attitude. Creative critical thinking leads to resolve. Think outside of any box with preconceived notions of life. Our differences allow us to be unique, varied and novel as human beings. The concept of the individual fuels the exchange and interchange of elements, originating from intimate and personal aspects of life. It is expressed through the culture, music and food shared across the globe. It is what makes the world go round. But what may work for one, may not work for all. This is where knowledge of self is most critical. Understanding yourself, and under what conditions you operate best, enables you to more effectively customize your life experience.

The Law of Vibrations states, "anything that exists in our universe, whether seen or unseen, broken down into and analyzed in its purest and most basic form, consists of pure energy or light which resonates and exists as a vibratory frequency or pattern. All matter thoughts and feelings have their own vibrational frequencies." Be aware of yourself and how you are received by others. 93% of the way we communicate has nothing to do with words. Also known as the 7/38/55 Rule rooted in studies by professor Albert Mehrabian in 1971. Referring to the primary forms of communication as body language and tone of voice. Be conscious of non-verbal communication. You will get back what you put out. Now that you're considering the value in individual life experiences, next time something happens, don't ask "why me?" All things work together, and we as individuals are part of the larger whole. We should all be humbled to take our individual places in this supreme collective of life.

Instead, let's start asking, "why not me?"

Volume I: Why Not You?

Di darkest part ah di night, ah when day soon light. ⇔ *The darkest part of the night is when day is soon light.*

When things and times are the hardest, brighter times are near.

Mental Break

(Final Thoughts)

What makes one person more valid than another?

Have you ever asked yourself "why me?" If so, when and why did you ask this?

Have you ever felt that someone else should endure a hardship that you may have experienced? If so, why?

Describe a bad situation you were able to receive something positive from:

What are you grateful for?

Rockstone ah rivah battam nuh know' sun hot. ⇔ Rocks at the bottom of the river don't know the sun is hot.

If you are sheltered, you do not know hardship.

Insights, opinions and notes: For you, by you.

A TRIBUTE TO MY INSPIRATION

Neon "Spoogy" Allen
Sunrise: November 28, 1993 – Sunset: December 2, 2016

The Caribbean Youth Club of Boston

I have watched you as individuals come together as one. I have witnessed the joy of a single person become cause for a group jam down. I have been at the graduations, celebrated at weddings, showered your babies and watched you elevate your careers. We have seen some of the best facets of life. We have also experienced some of the worst of them. But we've done it all together. This bond in our CYC family will last forever. Just remember, no matter where you go, or what you do, Ms. Keke will always be here and have lots of love for you.

"A smart person is not one that knows the answers, but one who knows where to find them!"

William Peterson

Marley musical inspiration for this volume is his 1980 song "Redemption Song."
Emancipate yourselves from mental slavery
None but ourselves can free our minds

**For more information on sessions with a Vision Life Consulting personal life coach,
email:** visionlifeservices@gmail.com

Testimonial Case Study
Tashalee Jackson and The Caribbean Youth Club

Issue/Dilemma:

High school aged youth who have recently migrated need supplemental supports. Often, they need more support than what is available in the classroom or at home. The President of the Caribbean Youth Club, Tashalee Jackson, provides insight and perspective. Ms. Jackson described the migration experience as "having to give up everything to move to a place with no friends and few family members."

The trauma associated with being separated from familiar supports is often exhibited by isolation, depression and lack of motivation in a young person. When individuals face this trauma, they often lose interest in societal expectations for success and high-level achievement. Keanna Green walked into the CYC with these evolved principles embedded in a once young and lonely girl of color in a classroom of physical non-identifiers.

Independent variable = Individual personal experience
Dependent variable = Successful individual transplanting to new cultures, communities, and geographical locations
Constant = Migration and individuals who engage in the process
Control = The Caribbean Youth Club. "Miss Keke" assisted programing execution. Concepts, notions, and processes explored in *Life's Reckoning*.

Concrete Examples:

Tashalee and all CYC members are tremendous examples of successful transplants. They were all born in foreign lands, with differing cultures. They have overcome those barriers to reap the fruits of their labor. Tashalee describes the prelude to her work with Keanna Green: "We were introduced to Keanna, otherwise known to us as Miss Keke. She was our mentor on relationships, life lessons and adjusting to a new place and country. Keke came on every trip, whether it was a dinner date with the CYC, a movie night, go-carting or driving to the Berkshires." By way of curriculum, guidance and mentoring from Keanna Green and Vision Life Consulting Services, students were able to grow as individuals and as a unit.

"Miss Keke passed on invaluable lessons to the students. She taught them that no one is worth losing their happiness over. That they would experience moments in which they would have to choose whether they would be living for someone else or themselves. She advised students to always choose themselves. Choose happiness. Choose peace of mind. Choose what would benefit them in the end. She left them with the powerful advice, "CHOOSE YOU!"

Tashalee sums up the current collective sentiment of CYC by explaining, "There will be times in your life when you will drift from the people that mean you good and want the best for you. You will end up losing your way. But, if you are like me, and you have the CYC and someone like Miss Keke, then you won't be lost for too long. They will come looking for you and guide you back to the path that you are supposed to be on. I am THANKFUL because I have them. Start looking now, find people in your life that you know will be there for you in ways that you never expect anyone to be.
BIG UP CYC! BIG UP Miss Keke!"

Final Thoughts from the Director:

Engaging others to be their best comes so naturally for Keanna Green. Words of praise and affirmation are her second language. That second language helped encourage me and over 50+ youth in Caribbean Youth Club to keep dreaming, growing and working to achieve greatness for the past 10 years. Keanna has a strong "ride or die" spirit that assures those who she supports that she is always in their corner. When you have a big idea, she doesn't shut it down; she probes about the implementation process. Then she lets out a loud, joyous, Jamaican laugh when she finds out the plans are unorthodox but workable.

It is from this deep well of optimism that she has written these workbooks. May her efforts in this series encourage you to reach your own level of greatness.
Blessings,

Nickey Nesbeth

Executive Director, Caribbean Youth Club

About the Author

I was born and raised in Boston, Massachusetts and spent many summers abroad in Jamaica. During my early years, I was surrounded by a small nuclear family (mom, dad, sister) and an overwhelmingly large extended family. The construct of my identity was established from birth, but continuously challenged throughout my life. My mom is American. My dad is Jamaican. Both firmly established in their own existences. My parents expected their children to embody strength, pride, and hard work. I was signed up for the METCO (Metropolitan Council for Educational Opportunity) program prior to reaching school age. For my family, METCO was the educational standard. Through the program, inner city students of color received the opportunity to attend public schools in surrounding, less diverse, suburban communities. I have cousins who either attended, or have graduated from, each of the participating towns in Massachusetts. We are all (for the most part) first generation Americans, born to ambitious immigrant parents from a tiny island in the Caribbean.

As a seven-year-old walking into Loker Elementary School, I embarked on a journey of daily migration alone. My new school community was located 16 miles and a 40 minute drive away from my home. As I walked into the school, I became aware of my existence. My existence of not only being a child of Kelly and Paul. But expounded, to include someone who is also black, urban, cultured via roots outside of the U.S., and considered to be of a lower class. I stood out like a sore thumb being the only person of color in the room. But I was excited. I had been conditioned to accept differences. My childhood was filled with exposure to different races and cultures. Being privy to white Jamaicans helped me accept differences of race, geography, culture, and people. I was ready to try something new and make new friends.

Wayland is an upper-middle class, suburban town west of Boston. It's a town culturally stuck in a time capsule. It resembles the *Leave it to Beaver* era of the 1950s. The school system had the intellectual challenges and scholastic resources afforded by affluence. Navigating these multiple worlds while maintaining a grounded sense of self was a challenge. A challenge I subconsciously took up, as a part of my life's mission and inspiration for my present work. I prevailed with the spirit of activism, which fueled my outspoken barrier busting resolve to issues my peers and I faced daily.

It all started with the flags. It was my first year at METCO. I did not have an issue with pledging allegiance to the American flag every day. However, I did have an issue looking around the school and only seeing the American flag as a representation of the student body. Flags and other visual symbols on school grounds should be inclusive and reflective of everyone. I had done my own bit of research. I found that there were other students who identified with roots outside of the U.S. I reasoned my issue with the principal during recess.

Today, there is a sea of flags in the auditorium. The Jamaican flag was the first flag hoisted into the rafters and sits right beside its American counterpart.

I graduated with a stronger sense of self. I knew that for most of the world, Black women were an afterthought. Yet, we are far more able, capable, and necessary than we will ever get credit for. A handful of staff, faculty and community organizers went out of their way to accommodate, assist and support the needs of the non-white students. These people saw the value in our voices during a time when most wanted us silenced — or even erased — from their suburban community.

I have always worked to share the knowledge, mentorship, guidance, discipline, care and love that I received during my development with others. I have shared these concepts and elements with hundreds of people within my community. I have also given back in a professional capacity. As a DTA (Department of Transitional Assistance) Recipient Lead Job Readiness and Life Skills Instructor with Career Team. As a worker with the Executive Office of Health and Human Services via DTA. As a business owner and life coach with Vision Life Consulting Services LLC. And as Assistant Program Administrator for the Caribbean Youth Club of Boston (CYC).

Working with CYC has been one of the most fulfilling professional experiences of my life. CYC was founded on some of the same principles as Loker Elementary. Principles such as maintaining cultural identity, excelling academically, and building tangible life skills. I am proud of the accomplishments and progress of all my CYC students. I have been blessed to watch them evolve and grow into responsible, creative, contributing members of society while maintaining their CYC family connection. I created this current project to help our CYC adolescent group as they encountered new experiences as adults. Before we could execute our plans, our chosen family suffered a loss. Neon Allen, a CYC student, mentor and developing programmer gained his angelic wings in a car accident. It happened days after his 23rd birthday.

We must work through grief and loss. They are mental and emotional constructs. That work has been different for all of us. Time has lapsed. It has been weeks, months or years since we have gotten together. Our future days will be brighter; I will see you there. My work was predetermined before I realized what it was. My great grandmother and grandmother were social workers. My father's mother had well over a hundred grand and great-grandchildren. It was a large family, but she took care of and maintained relationships with every member. Having access to strong personal, educational, professional, relatives, mentors and supports provided me with the best development. My network acts as my resource bank. A special thanks to all those who I have crossed paths with along my journey. Whether our relationship was positive, negative or indifferent, I see the accumulated wisdom as priceless. I have put a lot of time, effort and energy into this series. Keep an open mind as you move forward; you too may find the key to your future in your past! The work is done; the wait is over. Your reckoning is here!

Honorable Mention and Life Resource Recognition

In no official order

Glory be to the Most High who has secured my unending devotion to conscious connections with all, including self. The journey thus far has truly taught me what it means to walk by faith and not by sight. Thank you for your everlasting love, guidance, protection, and strength to carry me along my path when the road got rough. Forever humble. Forever grateful. Your simple servant.

My Mother: Kelly Smith – American ☺

To my mother, I love and appreciate you for all that you are. Your protective nature and supportive backing gives me strength.

A note to my American side: Growing up, I did not have the opportunity to see everyone much. But when I did, each moment was imprinted on my heart. I realized I wanted to be a social worker after a summer visit to Pine Bluff. Watching Nana performing welfare checks in the backwoods meant so much. Grammy, your incredible beauty, strength, compassion, and resolve resonates within me today, and I can see it in us all. Our past inspires me to continue pushing forward. We all have our lanes and I will see you in the future. Love and family always bring us back together. No matter the distance or the time, love always and forever.

My Father: "Paul" Green – Jamaican ☺

To my father, your determination to give me the best — and push me to be the best — continues to inspire me. You exposed me to a world outside of the one I was born into, and that has been a critical ingredient in my recipe for success.

A note to my Jamaican side: You were my every day and my all day. You were there for bad days and good grades. Through all the vacations and flights, birthdays, and holidays, we really did not fight. Basement made club tings, a long while, a "I just stop by fi gi yuh a joke" type thing. You are my childhood. My life's early education. I appreciate all that I have learned, and I respect our traditions. After more than forty years of annual summer trips, we have been through it all. Mama was the epitome of patience and love. A quiet strength who spoke louder than words. She never showed favor or excluded anyone with attention. She and Daddy Green built a solid foundation. Toya carried a sprit that can still be felt from above. She is with us every day, covering us with her love. Our shared experience in METCO made me feel less alone, during a time I was on a journey, all on my own. Thank you for exposing me to ways of the world and preparing me for life's ups, downs blessings, and blows. Memba, de love cyaan nevah done. **xoxo**

My Sister: Natale Green – Jamerican 😊 My up when I am down 😊

To my sister, my friend, my confidant. You are truly my physical balance in life. You have kept me grounded during life's storms when I could have been swept away. Peace and love be unto you always.

My niece Esmyra Montisol	Michelle Auterio
Marcus Montisol	Qwon Lynshue
Shantel Gillet	Merlene Barnes
Keon Williams	Michelle "Debbie" Henry
Aneesa Nichols	Daniel Johnson aka Mrs. Hot Sauce
Keyania Johnson	Mummy Delly
Kimberly Gabriel	Zion Earle
Ricaulder Augustine	Naiser Earle
Amy Afua	Uda Allen-Gunter
Tyisha Edwards	Nevado Earle
Denyse Mead	Mrs. Mabel Reid – Wallace
Sakina Flint	Mrs. Patricia Scully
Susan Flint	Cynthia Williams
	Ricardo Stewart

A special thank you to all three of my godfathers and both of my godmothers. Especially those who continue to play an active role in my life.

To Nickey Nesbeth and The Caribbean Youth Club of Boston: Thank you for becoming my chosen family. Your simple presence and positive vibes are irreplaceable to me. I knew after our first trip that the Most High was right. Being a blessing to another would be the ultimate blessing in my life. The learning process did not begin or end with any one of us. Over the years, you have given back and we have all learned so much. You all created the ideal atmosphere to educate, learn, be open, vulnerable, helpful and show praise. I will cherish your adolescents and those years of after school group. I'm still only a phone call away. I look forward to watching you all continue to evolve. I could never say enough how much I love you all.

Glossary

Acquired – To learn or develop (a skill, habit or quality)

Anxious pre-occupied attachment – Those possessing a negative view of self and positive view of others. Seeking high levels of intimacy, approval and responsiveness from their attachment figure

Assess – To evaluate or estimate the nature, ability or quality of

Asset – A useful or valuable thing, person or quality

Attachment style – Refers to the particular- way in which you relate to other people

Awareness – Knowledge or perception of a situation or fact

Babylon – Refers to a place of captivity as well as the power structure that enslaves

Barrier – An obstacle that prevents movement or access

Brimming – To be full of to the point of overflowing

Capacity – The maximum amount that something can contain

Chakra – (An Indian thought) Each of the centers of spiritual power in the human body. Usually considered to be seven in number

Co- dependent attachments – Refers to individuals who like to be in control and feed off the dependency of others. Often identify with being the "helper, rescuer, supporter or confidante"

Cognitive – Relating to the process of thinking and the identification of knowledge, as well as the understanding and the perception

Concept – An abstract idea, a general notion

Conceptualize – To form a concept or idea of

Confinement – The action of confining or restriction or a state of being confined or restricted

Connotation - An idea or feeling that a word invokes in addition to its literal or primary meaning

Conscious – Aware of and responding to one's surroundings; awake

Constructive - Serving a useful purpose; tending to build up

Commentary – An expression of opinions or offering of explanations about an event or situation

Correlation - A mutual relationship or connection between two or more things

Declaration – A formal or explicit statement or announcement

Dependent Attachments – Characterized by a strong need for validation from others, especially partners and friends. A seemingly natural giver but only a giver with the expectation of receiving the same in return.

Derailed – To obstruct (a process) by diverting it from it's intended course

Desensitized – Having been made less sensitive

Digestion – A person's capacity to break down substances that can be used for the individual

Disclaimer - A statement that denies something, especially responsibility

Discord – Disagreement between people

Dismissive Avoidant – Those possessing a positive view of self and a negative view of others. The desire for independence often appears as an attempt to avoid attachment all together. Tend to suppress and hide and deal with rejection by distancing themselves

Displacement – The moving of something from its place or position

Disposition – A person's inherent quality of mind and character

Diversify – Enlarge or vary the range products or the field of operation of a business

Duality – An instance of opposition or contrast between two concepts of something.

Enhance – Intensify, increase, or further improve the quality, value or extent of

Endure – To remain in existence; to last

Enlightened – Having or showing a rational, modern, and well-informed outlook

Envision – imagine as a future possibility

Equitable - Fair and impartial

Essence – The intrinsic nature or indispensable quality of something, especially something abstract that determines its character

Essential – Absolutely necessary; extremely important

Evaluation – The making of a judgement about the amount, number, or value of something

Execute – Carry out or put into effect (plan, order or course of action)

Exhibit – To manifest or deliberately display (a quality or type or behavior)

Expendable income – income that you have left over after taxes, bills, food etc has been bought

Expose - reveal the true, objectionable nature of (someone or something)

External – Something on the outside of a surface or body that exists, happens or comes from the outside

Factor – A circumstance, fact or influence that contributes to a result or outcome

Fearful Avoidant – Possessing an unstable fluctuating / confused view of self and others. Seek less intimacy from attachments and frequently suppress and deny their feelings. Loss and trauma such as sexual abuse in childhood and adolescence may develop this type of attachment

Forecast – To predict or estimate

Forthcoming – Planned for or about to happen in the future

Fortified – Provided with defensive works as a protection against attack

Fruition – The point at which a plan or project is realized

Gravitate – Moving forward or be attracted to a place, person or thing

Holistic – Characterized by the treatment of the whole person, taking into account mental and social factors, rather than just the symptoms of a disease

Humility – A modest or low view of one's own importance

Illuminate – To light up

Impartial – Treating all rivals or disputes equally; fain and just

Implicate / Imply – Convey (a meaning or intention) indirectly through what one says rather than stating it explicitly

Inalienable Rights – Personal rights held by an individual, which are not bestowed by law, custom or belief, and which cannot be taken or given away.

Incumbent – Necessary (for someone) as a duty or responsibility

Indifferent – Having no particular interest or sympathy; unconcerned

Inequity – Lack of fairness or justice

Infatuation – An intense but short-lived passion or admiration for someone or something

Infectious – Likely to spread or influence others in a rapid manner

Insecurity – Uncertainty or anxiety about one's self; lack of confidence

Inside – out method – The process of mental and emotional digestions for life management. Founded in the balanced awareness of one's self via both internal and external factors. Developed by vision life consulting services LLC

Intangible – Unable to be touched or grasped; not having physical presence

Investment – The act of spending or using money with the expectation of achieving a profit

Jamerican – An American of Jamaican birth or ancestry

Landscape – All the visible features of an area or land

Legacy – The Amount of money or property left to someone in a will

Management – The process of dealing with or controlling things or people

Manifest – To display or show (a quality or feeling) by one's acts or appearance; demonstrate

Market – An area in which commercial dealings are conducted

Merely – Just; only

Meticulous – Showing a great attention to detail; very careful and precise

Mitigate – To lessen the gravity of an offense or mistake

Mortal – A human being subject to death

Mundane – Lacking interest or excitement; dull

Net – The sum or difference of two or more variables

Neutral – Not helping or supporting either side in a conflict or discord

Neutralizer – To make neutral

Notion – A Conception of or belief about something

Objective – A thing aimed at or sought; a goal

Optimistic – Hopeful and confident about the future

Par – The face value (Stock); the number of strokes required for a particular golf course

Parameters – A numerical or other measurable factor (one or apart of a set) that defines a system or sets the conditions of its operation

Paramount – More important than anything else; Supreme

Perpetuate – Make something continue indefinitely

Perspective – A particular attitude toward or way of regarding something; a point of view

Plot – A plan made in secret

PMA (positive mental attitude)– A mental and emotional state of wellbeing

Portfolio – A range of investments held by a person or organization

Prerequisite – A thing that is required as a prior condition for something else to happen or exist

Presumed – Suppose that something is the case basis of probability

Primitive – Relating to the early to the early stage in the evolutionary or historical development of something

Profound – (A person or statement) Having or showing great knowledge or insight

Projection – An estimate or forecast of a future situation or trend based on a study of present ones

Proverb – A short saying in general use, stating a general truth or piece of advice

Reckoning – The action or process of calculating something

Redemption – The action of saving or being saved from sin, error or evil

Refinement – The process of removing impurities or unwanted element from a substance

Replicate – Make a close or exact copy

Reside – To belong by right

Resonate – (derived from resonance a common vibration) Two things move in unison

Retain – Continue to have (something); Keep possession of

Secure Attachment – Possessing a positive view of self as well as a positive view of others. Feeling comfortable with both intimacy and independence.

Solitude – The state or situation of being alone

Stagnant – Showing no activity dull and sluggish

Stake – Mark an area to claim ownership of

Stride – A step or stage in process toward an aim

Subconscious – Of or concerning the part of the mind of which one is not fully -aware but which influences one's actions and feelings

Supplemental – Provided in addition to what is already present or available to complete or enhance it

Tangible – Perceptible by touch

Transcend – Be or go beyond the range of limits

Trajectory – The path followed, moving under the action of given forces

Unsolicited – Not asked for; given or done freely

Vested – Secured in the possession of or assigned to a person

Via – By way of

Virtue – Behavior showing high moral standards

Vivid – Producing powerful feelings or strong clear images in the mind

Warrant – Justification or authority for an action belief or feeling

www.ingramcontent.com/pod-product-compliance
Lightning Source LLC
Chambersburg PA
CBHW082041080526
44578CB00009B/797